SHEET MUSIC *for* PIANO

Scarlatti

Intermediate to Advanced Piano Masterpieces

MP3s
ONLINE LINKS
Resources

Alan Brown

With an Introduction by Michael J. West

FLAME TREE
PUBLISHING

FLAME TREE
PIANO & KEYBOARD

Publisher and Creative Director: Nick Wells
Commissioning Editor: Polly Prior
Project Editor: Gillian Whitaker
Music Transcription: Alan Brown
Introductory Text: Michael J. West

This edition first published 2019 by
FLAME TREE PUBLISHING
6 Melbray Mews
Fulham, London SW6 3NS
United Kingdom
www.flametreepublishing.com
www.flametreemusic.com

Website for this book: www.flametreepiano.com

© 2019 Flame Tree Publishing Ltd

19 21 23 22 20
1 3 5 7 9 10 8 6 4 2

ISBN 978-1-78755-779-6

A CIP record for this book is available from the British Library upon request.

Alan Brown (Music Transcription)
A former member of the Scottish National Orchestra, Alan now works as a freelance
musician with several leading UK orchestras, and as a consultant in music and IT. Alan has
had several compositions published, developed a set of music theory CD-Roms, co-written a
series of Bass Guitar Examination Handbooks and worked on over 100 further titles.

Michael J. West (Introductory Text)
Michael J. West is a jazz critic and journalist, a contributor to *JazzTimes*, *DownBeat*, the
Washington Post, the *Washington City Paper*, *JAZZIZ* and *Bandcamp Daily*. His work has also
appeared in *Slate*, *NPR Music*, WAMU.org, *The Village Voice*, *The Jazz Cruise* newsletter, *East
Bay Express*, and others. He lives in Washington with his wife and two children, who fill his
heart with joy by requesting Thelonious Monk and Duke Ellington albums at bedtime.

Images © the following: 6 World History Archive/SuperStock; 7 DeAgostini/SuperStock;
8 INTERFOTO/TopFoto; 10 Yale University Art Gallery, New Haven, CT, USA/Bridgeman
Images; 11 Luisa Ricciarini/Bridgeman Images.

Printed in China

Contents

Intermediate Piano Pieces 🌿

Advanced Piano Pieces 🌿

How to Use the Website

The Flame Tree Piano and Keyboard website (flametreepiano.com) offers a number of significant benefits for readers and users of this sheet music book. It can be accessed on a desktop computer (Mac or PC), tablet (such as the iPad or Nexus) or any internet-enabled smartphone.

The Home Page

With a series of options the website allows the reader to find out more, both about the composer and the music. Biographies, mp3s and further resources are provided to allow you to explore the subject further.

The Audio Player

The primary tool on the website is the use of an audio player. All the pieces are presented to help you understand each of the masterpieces in this book. The simple play ▶ button allows you to play each piece through the speakers on your device. Although the music cannot be downloaded, it is streamed and is provided free of charge.

Life and Works

This book of sheet music pieces for the piano is introduced with a short guide to the composer. The website presents a more extensive text on the life, works, style and context, with information extracted from *The Classical Music Encyclopedia* (Flame Tree Publishing), edited by Stanley

Sadie (1930–2005), with a foreword by Vladimir Ashkenazy. Music editor for *The Times* for 17 years and editor of the standard classical music reference work *The New Grove Dictionary of Music and Musicians*, Stanley Sadie was, amongst many other achievements, president of the Royal Musical Association and the International Musicological Society. (*The Classical Music Encyclopedia* will be republished online and made available as a downloadable pdf, from www.flametreepiano.com.)

Free eBook

Created to complement this new series of books we have made a special edition, 96-page ebook, *Romantic Composers*. Featuring the primary composers, musicians and musical artists of the Romantic Era, the ebook can be downloaded onto any computer, tablet or smartphone and is an invaluable source of reference on a key period of musical history.

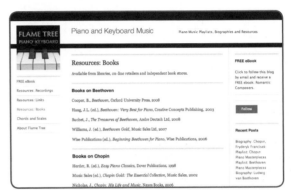

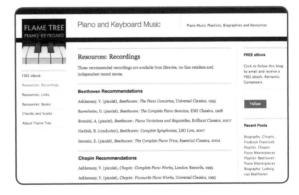

Other Features

The experience of playing the piano is one of constant development. To help with further discoveries we have provided a number of additional resources. Separate menus offer recommendations for further reading (books and online) and particular recordings.

Introduction to Domenico Scarlatti

The stars seemed aligned from his birth for Domenico Scarlatti's (1685–1757) greatness as a composer. The son of Alessandro Scarlatti, a composer of vocal music and the greatest figure of the Neapolitan School of opera, he was also born in the same year as both Johann Sebastian Bach and George Frideric Handel. Nevertheless, this youngest Scarlatti (his elder brother, Pietro Filippo Scarlatti, was also a composer) startled the musical establishment of Europe's Baroque era with his genius, both at the keyboard and the writing desk.

As expected, Scarlatti did indeed write a few operas, as well as chamber cantatas and church music. However, it is his works for keyboard – written for harpsichord, but easily translated to piano – on which Scarlatti's reputation rests. Although only a relative handful of his compositions were published during his lifetime, they were hailed for their virtuosity and originality, and were benchmarks in the transition from the Baroque to the classical style. In the 250 years since his death, the number of Scarlatti's known and published keyboard sonatas has swelled to 550, a corpus that is today regarded as among the finest ever produced.

To the Manner Born

The Scarlattis were perhaps the first family of music in the Kingdom of Naples when Domenico was born there. (Along with his father, Domenico's uncle Francesco was also a composer and violinist of note.) Though little has been documented of his youthful training, it is assumed that he first studied with members of the family – especially his father, whose heavy hand would prove difficult to shake.

Whatever the case, his talent and skill developed to such a degree that by the age of 15 he had been appointed composer and organist at the royal chapel in Naples. Despite his prodigious abilities at keyboard, however, the elder Scarlatti wished his son to pursue vocal music first and foremost; Domenico had at least two of his own operas produced in Naples during 1703–04. In 1705, however, Alessandro arranged for the 19-year-old to travel to Venice and study with the opera composer Francesco Gasparini.

The years 1705–08, probably coinciding with Scarlatti's time in Venice, represents another undocumented period in his life. He probably studied with Gasparini, and reputedly with Gaetano Greco and Bernardo Pasquini as well; he may also have met George Frideric Handel, whom he would encounter again.

Success in Rome

What is certain is that in spring 1709, Scarlatti arrived in Rome, the centre of what was then the Papal States, to enter into the employment (probably obtained through his father's machinations) of Marie Casimire, the exiled former queen of Poland. The successful 1710 performance of his opera *La Silvia* at the queen's theatre began a run of seven operatic successes and cemented her patronage of the young harpsichordist and composer. By 1711, he had been appointed Marie Casimire's *maestro di cappella* (musical director), under which auspices he composed and probably performed at least one (surviving) oratorio and one cantata for her.

Title page for Scarlatti's *Exercises for the Harpsichord (Volume A)*

18th Century Copper Engraving of a Concert Given by Domenico Scarlatti and Other Italian Composers

The Polish queen left Rome in 1714. Shortly thereafter, Scarlatti became *maestro* of the Cappella Giulia (the chapel of St. Peter's Basilica at the Vatican), where he was charged with composing and performing liturgical and occasional compositions. In 1715 Rome's Teatro Capricano commissioned him to write operas (though he would only complete one by himself). He additionally continued composing cantatas and other pieces, including a serenade that he premiered at the Portuguese embassy in 1714.

However, he also continued to be dominated by his father, frustrating his increasing attention to instrumental music. In 1709 he had famously engaged Handel in a contest on both the harpsichord and the organ, with Scarlatti triumphing on the former instrument. He gained a reputation throughout Rome as a great virtuoso of the harpsichord. Yet he was apparently unable to pursue this avenue freely because of Alessandro's insistence that opera be his focus (and interference to that end). Not until 1717, when he was 32 years old, was he able to obtain legal independence from the elder Scarlatti.

The Portuguese Princess

Scarlatti's 1714 serenade performance at the Embassy of Portugal had won him the attention – and ultimately the patronage – of the Portuguese ambassador, the Marques de Fontes. He resigned his position at the Vatican in late 1719, apparently bound for

London but instead arriving in Lisbon. The Marques quickly secured him a position as musical master at the court of King João V. In that capacity he again served as master of the royal chapel, composing religious cantatas, oratorios, serenades and liturgical pieces. (Notably, he composed no operas after leaving Rome.) More importantly, he also became the music teacher for the royal family, with Princess Maria Barbara – nine years old when she began her studies – as his primary harpsichord pupil.

It was at this time that Scarlatti turned his attention to creating music for keyboard. Primarily this took the form of lessons and exercises for his students, who, in addition to the royal household, included composer Carlos Seixas. (Some sources suggest that Seixas introduced Scarlatti to the Portuguese folk music that would later become a prominent influence in his sonatas.) Most of these pieces, however, were probably written for the princess, who Scarlatti discovered to have a formidable musical talent.

Indeed, as she developed her ability on the instrument, Scarlatti's career became inextricably tied to her progress. Much to his good fortune, Maria Barbara became increasingly devoted to playing music – and to her master. In 1729, she married the heir to the throne of Spain and invited Scarlatti to follow her to her adopted country.

The musician first moved to Seville, remaining there for four years. In 1733 Scarlatti joined Maria Barbara at the Spanish court in Madrid, where he remained in her employment for the rest of his life.

Spain and the Sonatas

Although he lived as a servant of Bourbon dynastic family in Madrid, Scarlatti also maintained his salary from King João V of Portugal, since he remained the teacher of the princess. (He was even made a knight by João in 1738.) Although he continued to teach, he was primarily the beneficiary of a single patroness – one who could support him with the wealth of two kingdoms.

Scarlatti became the de facto court composer for Maria Barbara and her husband, the future Fernando VI, writing music for state functions, royal banquets and other social events. (These became increasingly opulent, with corresponding demands on the music, after they became King and Queen of Spain in 1746.) Fernando and Maria Barbara also made opera increasingly fashionable in Spanish society, with Scarlatti undoubtedly assisting with productions and conducting orchestras. However, he still declined to compose any new operas. He did befriend and collaborate with the castrato singer Farinelli, who came to Madrid in 1737, yet a few cantatas written for Farinelli seem to constitute his entire compositional output of vocal music from his life in Spain.

Instead, Scarlatti wrote massive amounts of music for his longtime student. Maria Barbara had never ceased refining her talents on the harpsichord, and after he settled into Madrid, Scarlatti began writing single-movement sonatas for her to practise and perform in private royal concerts. (The compositions are undated, and any sort of chronology is highly problematic; however, evidence indicates that Scarlatti's entire body of keyboard sonatas was written after 1735.) He published 30 of them in 1738 as a collection entitled *Essercizi*, which was received with awe and rapturous praise – particularly in England, where the critic Charles Burney and composer Thomas Roseingrave hailed him as a genius.

The bulk of Scarlatti's other (especially vocal) compositions are regarded as serviceable but unexceptional, with a few pieces hinting at greater promise for their author. The

The Court of Ferdinand VI of Spain and Maria Barbara, engraving after Jacopo Amigoni (c. 1675–1752)

sonatas, however, seem to have been written by a very different and highly sophisticated composer. No doubt attempting to challenge the Queen and her increasingly assured prowess at the keyboard, Scarlatti experimented with structures and substructures, shifting textures, as well as modalities, dissonances and other atypical harmonic devices. The pieces moved away from the Baroque elaborations of the period and toward a cleaner, more elegant conception that would become known as the 'galant' style (from which evolved the music of the classical period).

He also made novel use of the traditional musics of the Iberian peninsula, incorporating the rhythms and phrasing of the peasant chants, gypsy minstrels and folk dances of Spain and Portugal. A number of his sonatas even feature passagework that imitates the Spanish guitar.

Posthumous Discovery

There are 550 known Scarlatti sonatas. The overwhelming majority of them remained unpublished in Scarlatti's lifetime. He seems to have intended to publish them, having spent much of his final few years meticulously organizing the sonatas into manuscript volumes. Yet when he died on 23 July 1757, only the 30 sonatas of Scarlatti's 1738 *Essercizi* had been revealed to the world.

Frontispiece for Scarlatti's First Volume of Harpsichord Pieces

Even then, the work did not surface in published form for another eight decades. The great pianist Franz Liszt reintroduced Scarlatti to the music world in the late 1830s when he began including the known sonatas in his concerts and recitals. The Austrian composer and teacher Carl Czerny finally published a substantial portion of them in 1839; a mostly complete collection appeared in 1906, with scattered pieces surfacing in the time since. By the end of the 20th century, Domenico Scarlatti's keyboard sonatas had become an essential component of the western musical canon.

K 1

Allegro

K 7

Allegretto

K 9

Allegretto

K 27

Allegro

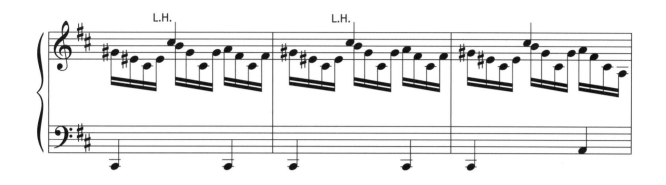

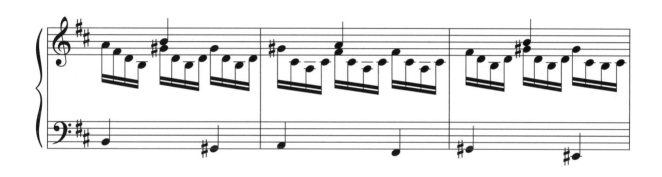

K 30

Allegro

K 33

Allegro

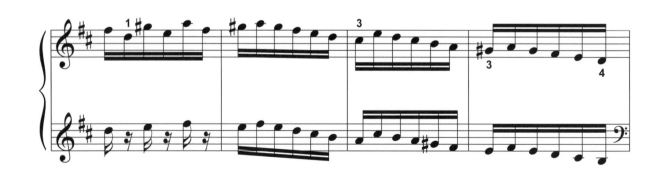

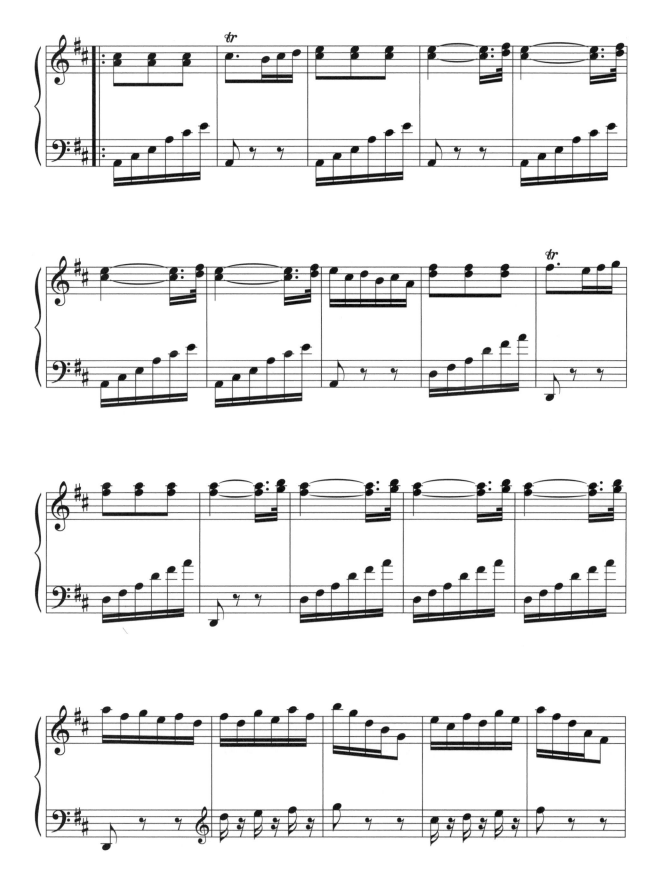

K 43

Allegro

K 67

Allegro

K 119

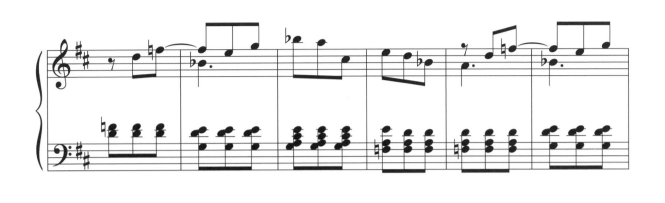

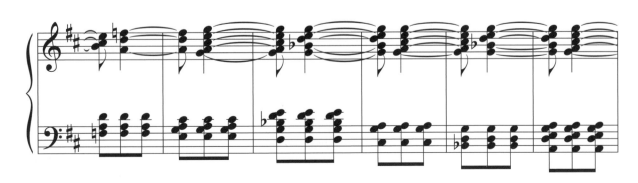

K 146

Allegro

K 147

K 151

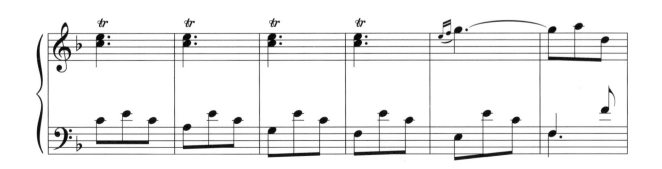

K 158

K 159

Allegretto

K 202

Allegro

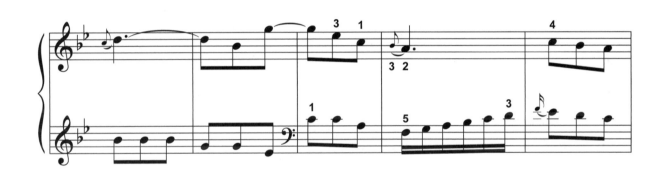

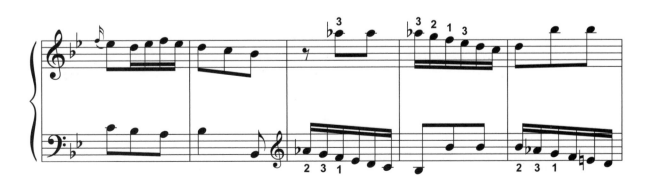

K 208

K 239

K 296

K 380

Allegro

K 456

Allegro

K 461

Allegro

K 467

Allegro

K 491

Allegro

K 535

www.flametreepiano.com

Audio playlists with the pieces from this book.

Comprehensive biography of Domenico Scarlatti.

Free eBook: *Romantic Composers.*

Resource links to books and internet sites.

Recommended recordings.